MW00975202

Winning Your First Client

Understanding Selling in Practice

Martin Bissett

LIBRARY DATA
Bissett, Martin
CPA Trendlines, an imprint of Bay Street Group LLC

ISBN-13: 978-0982714706
ISBN-10: 098271470X

BISAC: Business & Economics / Accounting / General
1. Accounting firms – Marketing
2. Accounting firms – Management
3. Accounting firms – United States

Table of Contents

Dear Reader,

Whenever you pick up a book that promotes a certain approach, methodology, technique or ethos, as this one does, the front of the book is packed with sentiments like...

'Martin has some very insightful ideas and I now have a much better idea of how to structure meetings when trying to win work and also how to have a much more structured follow-up approach after such meetings....'

'We recently started working with Martin as our sales process just wasn't working as it should do. Already after two sessions we have started seeing very positive changes and implemented some of Martin's excellent ideas. His enthusiasm and skill really rubs off on our.....'

'Martin has already transformed our approach to Business Development. Not only has he demonstrated how best to approach our marketing process but he has also helped us with the practical implementations....'

'Martin has real in-depth knowledge of his speciality, which is sales and marketing for accountants. He has shown a real interest in our practice and goals and ensured that our ethics correspond to his own, and has helped us break down barriers and build relationships with potential clients....'

etc etc etc .

Don't get me wrong, the above are real examples of endorsements written by real clients, and I am greatly indebted to those who wrote them, but you'd hardly expect to read anything else other than high praise would you?

So instead of filling this page with endorsements that you'd presume I'd have plenty of anyway, how about we do things a little differently?

How about I offer my thanks to you for giving of your time to read this book, that I invite you to consider its content, reflect on how it might positively impact you and your firm and then encourage you to have a go at implementing the content found in these pages?

If that implementation leads to clear, discernible, sustained and positive improvement in your efforts to grow the firm, you have a better endorsement for this book and series than I could ever put on paper from other people's words.

To your success!

Martin Bissett

Foreword

It's been 16 years since I started working with the accounting profession. I have sat in over a thousand partners' offices in that time, worked with roughly half of
that number and been a part of delivery teams who have
created over £450m worth of new opportunities for those
firms.

In that time, I have witnessed the highs and the lows of
business development in the profession. I've seen the
common vernacular of business owners downgrade
Accounting from a once noble 'profession' to a mere 'in-
dustry'. I have also seen what the best firms do to win
high-end work, at high-end fees and in short turnaround
times. The common denominator in those firms is that
their partners win their first client on a daily basis.

'Winning your first client' refers to a state of mind that
we adopt before ever speaking to prospective new clients.
A common concern raised to me by partners of accounting firms is that they are unsure they can offer anything
above and beyond that which a potential client is already
receiving from their current accountant.

If we don't know how we can provide superior support
to the business we want to win as a client, we really can't
expect our prospective clients to know that either.

Understand Selling In Practice by Knowing:

'Winning Your First Client' refers to a state of mind that we adopt before ever speaking to prospective new clients.

Winning your first client is all about understanding why someone would buy from you before you ever speak to them, before you ever start the preparation for talking to them.

Therefore, winning your first client is all about understanding why someone would buy from you before you ever speak to them, before you ever meet them, before you ever start the preparation for talking to them.

I find that this discipline goes unexplained by most 'sales training' offered to the accounting profession, but ultimately we have to be comfortable with who we are and the value that we offer.

We have to be comfortable with such little details as our appearance, the way we speak, the way we come across, the strength of the handshake, the amount of eye contact. All of these tiny little nuances play a part in how we are perceived by our prospective clients when we go and see them, or when they come and see us. So the more we can get in order first, the more relaxed and natural we are, which allows us to build the relationship we referred to in the introduction.

In case it's not clear yet, the 'First Client' is YOU. 'Winning Your First Client' is therefore the concept and practice of understanding why your accounting firm can bring more value to the table for a business than they get from their current accountants. It is about understanding that you must be perceived as professional, that you must be punctual, that you must understand the business owner's personal needs, which drive their business's needs.

Understand Selling In Practice by Knowing:

If we don't know how we can provide superior support to the business we want to win as a client, we really can't expect our prospective clients to know that either.

The 'First Client' is YOU!

Ultimately, this can be summed up in one question: "If we were to meet us, would we be impressed with ourselves to the extent of wanting to work together?"

Perhaps your personal modesty doesn't allow you to admit that you would be impressed with yourself, but in selling our professional services we all need that kind of assurance, because once we have confidence about how we come across, we are much more assured, and able to project that image to prospective clients as well.

Understand Selling In Practice by Knowing:

If we were to meet us, would we be impressed with ourselves to the extent of wanting to work together?

U.S.P. Points to Ponder

Why have your currently existing clients chosen to work with you ahead of the competition?

_____
_____
_____
_____
_____
_____
_____
_____

Introduction

Have you noticed all of those titles in the local bookstore or at the airport offering us the 'key' to this and the 'key' to that, the 'six keys' to one thing and the 'four keys' to another?

It also seems that every book is a 'game-changer' now, to the point where it is difficult to understand what the game is any more, never mind how to play it.

When it comes to winning new work in professional services, we must first build a relationship. The game hasn't changed at all in that respect.

In this guidebook, I too offer you a 'key', but the key is worthless unless the key holder places it in the lock and turns it in the right direction. This key is a 'game changer' for anyone who doesn't currently use it, but since you now know that I don't like that term, I'll use 'consistently proven' instead.

However, should you choose to use this key as directed in this guidebook, you will very quickly learn the secret, the master key to business development.

Okay you get the idea. So what is this key? Well, it's nothing new, nothing ground-breaking. It is simply the

Understand Selling In Practice by Knowing:

It's not having the key...

It's using the key daily that opens doors for you

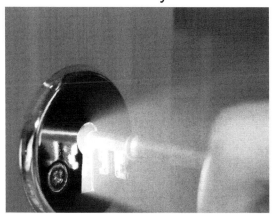

process of overcoming a condition long known as FTI (failure to implement.)

That is where we always go wrong with business development. It's not a case of not doing any business development work. Lots of firms go out there and market and then try and sell to their prospects. It's not a lack of implementation, it's a lack of *correct* implementation —the knowledge of what to do and how to implement it in the correct order and in the correct way.

Most of us still rely on referrals coming in the door to build our practices and our portfolios. We augment this with a little bit of networking and a little bit of marketing, but a proactive push which is measured, monitored and scientifically created is something that most of us don't do.

So by overcoming the failure to correctly implement proactive preparation, which you will learn in these pages, you'll beat the vast majority of firms you'll ever come up against.

The secret to overcoming failure to correctly implement a successful business development strategy is by 'winning your first client' (which will be explained) and this starts by being accountable to someone for your performance.

Understand Selling In Practice by Knowing:

The secret to overcoming failure to correctly implement a successful business development strategy is by 'winning your first client' and this starts by being accountable to someone for your performance.

USP Points to Ponder

Who are you prepared to be accountable to for your business development results?

Now that 'someone' may be your fellow partners in the firm; if you are a senior manager, that may be the partner to whom you report. If you're a sole practitioner or if you don't find being accountable to your partners helpful, then you can be accountable to your life partner, spouse or another person you wouldn't want to see you fail.

So we get that push from being accountable to someone, someone we want to make sure is impressed by what we do, that we don't want to fall foul of. That is how we overcome failure to implement in a very, very simple way.

Once we're prepared to do that, we can start the process of winning our first client.

What follows are the *8 Pieces of Value* which empower you to do just that.

Understand Selling In Practice by Knowing:

8 Pieces of Value Questions to Master:

1. Do you create an impressive perception of yourself and your firm to prospective client?
2. Do you consider yourself successful in life?
3. Do you set yourself up to win on a daily basis?
4. Do you find differentiating yourself and your firm from your competitors to be easy?
5. Do you chase new fees or do you attract them?
6. Do you discount and low-ball your fees to win work?
7. Do you set aside specific non-interruptible time to work on business development efforts on a weekly basis?
8. Do you sell on price or on value?

1st Piece of Value – Perception is Reality

As far as our potential clients are concerned, how they perceive us is how we really are to them, regardless of the truth of the matter.

Because of this, it's important to realise that when we are meeting a new potential client who has *not* been referred to us, it does not matter what the reality of our value proposition is; it matters how that potential client perceives our value proposition. Therefore, to be effective in winning work, we must understand how we can positively influence their perception of us at each stage of the relationship-building process.

One of the many myths that we have around business development in the accounting profession is that because we've never been trained to sell and because we struggle to sell, this means that we cannot sell. That's not true. That's a myth. Any frailty in mastering a process is a matter of a lack of understanding, not a lack of ability.

At the time of writing, I can't fly a fighter plane and I can't perform a tax computation with anything like the degree of ability that my accounting firm clients can. I am sufficiently self-assured, however, that I know I have a reasonable level of intelligence and I can learn to do

Understand Selling In Practice by Knowing:

One of the many myths that we have around business development in the accounting profession is that because we've never been trained to sell and because we struggle to sell, this means that we cannot sell. That's not true. That's a myth.

"No man has the ability to step outside of the shadow of his own character." — Robespierre

---

those seemingly impossible things once I know the framework and the process and I get the process right.

The promising sign is that 87% of the firms I have spoken to in preparation for writing this guidebook have said they don't see selling as something they can't do. That's encouraging but leaves me feeling acutely aware that the other 13% of those who may read this do see 'selling' as something they can't do.

Selling is simply a process which is executed most effectively when we believe in ourselves.

Understand Selling In Practice by Knowing:

The promising sign is that 87% of the firms I have spoken to in preparation for writing this guidebook have said they don't see selling as something they can't do.

Selling is simply a process which is executed most effectively when we believe in ourselves.

2nd Piece of Value – Those Successful in Winning New Work Are Generally Successful In Life First

So now you know the identity of your first client, and if you buy into you, there's a good chance of potential clients being prepared to do so too.

This is what we must remember about the purchasing of professional services such as accounting. If your prospective client is a Grade A or B style opportunity for your firm, then they are not buying the services you provide *per se*. The services are the vehicles of delivery; the means to the end. The client is buying the relationship, and they are asking themselves

- 'Do I like this person?'

- 'Can I get on with this person?'

- 'Do I want this person to advise my business? and

- 'Do I believe they can can help me to advance my business more than my current accountant can?'

How do we determine whether we are the kind of person that someone else would buy from?

Understand Selling In Practice by Knowing:

If your prospective client is a Grade A or B style opportunity for your firm, then they are not buying the services you provide per se. *The services are the vehicles of delivery, the means to the end. The client is buying the relationship.*

U.S.P. Points to Ponder

What outcome do you deliver for your clients?

I've put together a short criterion which is a general overview of what is in place in the successful person's life. This may or may not be an appropriate measure for you, but hopefully you will see how successful business developers puts their own personal 'house' in order first before presenting themselves to the general public.

If I were to ask you the following questions today, how would you answer them?

Do you like how you've treated your family members recently?

Because this will play on your mind until it is resolved.

Have you been striving to hit any personal goals that you've made for yourself?

In January, of course, there's always New Years' resolutions that generally involve losing weight or earning more money or changing jobs or something like that, and the goal is usually gone by March (or the second week in January). So if you are striving to hit personal goals that you've set yourself, regardless of whether you're hitting them or not, making that effort will instill a sense of pride within yourself. You can say, "Yeah, I'm working hard to improve something about myself," or "Yeah, I'm being the kind of person I want to be."

Understand Selling In Practice by Knowing:

Successful business developers put their own personal 'house' in order first before presenting themselves to the general public.

If you are striving to hit personal goals that you've set yourself, regardless of whether you're hitting them or not, making that effort will instill a sense of pride within yourself.

That translates into the enthusiasm and the assuredness with which you present yourself to a prospective client.

How have you dealt with your employees and clients recently?

If it was shown back to you on a video, would you be happy with what you saw? What you included on the timesheet when no one could see you—how does that reflect on your personal level of integrity? Your professional conduct, believe it or not, intangible as it might be, translates into how you are perceived by potential clients; and their perception is their reality, so it's the only thing you need to worry about.

Are you happy with the way you present yourself visually?

Are you a shirt and tie kind of person? Are you a little bit more casual than that, do you shave, do you not shave? How do you look? If you were meeting yourself for the first time, what would be your first impression of the person who walks through the door?

Are you happy with how you present yourself verbally?

Do you mutter, do you slur your speech for whatever reason? Do you enunciate very clearly, do you gesticulate? Are you very animated?

Understand Selling In Practice by Knowing:

Your professional conduct, believe it or not, intangible as it might be, translates into how you are perceived by potential clients.

If you were meeting yourself for the first time, what would be your first impression of the person who walks through the door?

Are you happy with the quality of work you and your team produce?

When you tell potential clients you can solve their problems, are you saying that because you think it's what they want to hear, or are you just giving it as a statement of fact because you know you have a library of case studies that show you've done tremendous work for your clients?

Do you like yourself to the extent that if you met you, you'd be impressed?

Yes or no? If no, what needs to be done to make it a yes?

Do you like how much preparation you've invested in each meeting?

Do you know only what is claimed on the prospect's website, or has your interest in their business allowed you to carry out some more impressive fact finding?

Believe it or not, the above are all factors in how we're perceived by our clients and prospects, and they are very rarely talked about in discussions about business development. People buy relationships, and people buy the outcomes produced by those relationships.

Understand Selling In Practice by Knowing:

When you tell potential clients you can solve their problems, are you saying that because you think it's what they want to hear, or are you just giving it as a statement of fact because you know you have a library of case studies that show you've done tremendous work for your clients?

People buy relationships, and people buy the outcomes produced by those relationships.

All these things go into the general mix of how we perceive ourselves and therefore how our clients perceive us.

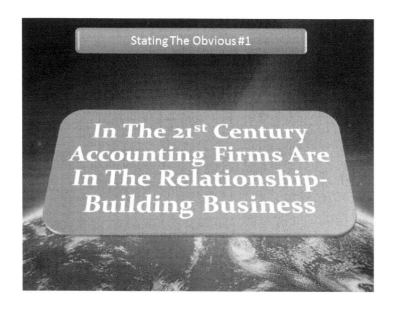

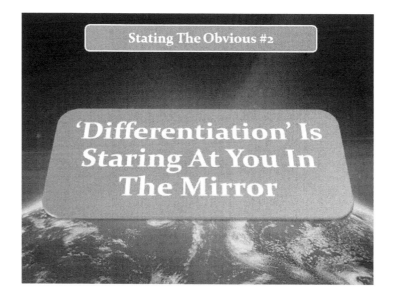

3rd Piece of Value – Win Your First Client _Daily_

Being a successful person according to your own measurement of that and your own goals and your own standards, is different for everyone.

If you're comfortable with you, it's very likely that others will be too. If you understand the value that you offer (how you can improve a client's situation to move them closer towards their personal and professional aspirations) you're likely to be able to convey that value in front of a prospect. That's a huge part of successful business development which is not often talked about.

What if you feel that 'selling' is stigmatised in the accounting profession?

For the 70% of accounting firm partners I've spoken to over the years who feel that there is a stigma attached to having to 'sell' their professional services, I would like to change the word selling in your minds to one of two things, whichever one you prefer. Either 'relationship building' or 'business developing'. Business Developing or selling is essentially a process of building a relationship that's going to last forever and that's what we want to create a perception of with our clients.

Understand Selling In Practice by Knowing:

If you're comfortable with you, it's very likely that others will be too.

For the 70% of accounting firm partners I've spoken to over the years who feel that there is a stigma attached to having to 'sell' their professional services, I would like to change the word selling in your minds to one of two things, whichever one you prefer. Either 'relationship building' or 'business developing'.

We don't want them for a year (unless they're particularly hard work)—we want them for as long as possible. We want those recurring fees coming in, as it's how we build our own personal wealth.

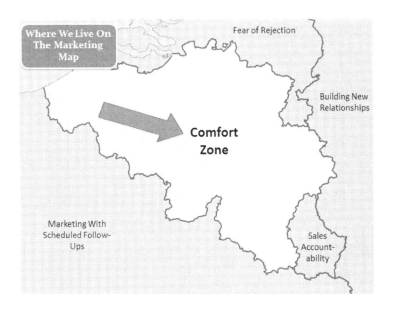

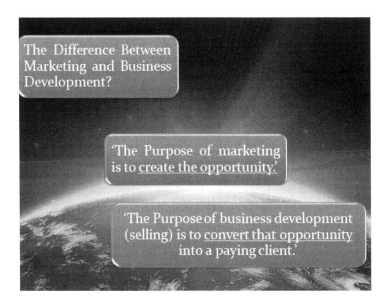

4th Piece of Value – It Is No Longer Difficult To Sell Accounting Services

Let's take a look at the last 16 years of my experience and my research as to where new clients come from in an accounting practice. I don't think there's going to be too many shocks here.

What I've found is that 82% of all new clients in a given year that come into an accounting firm come in from a referral source. This may be a bank or a lawyer or some other source, perhaps an existing client, who has recommended that a particular business meet with your firm and come on board as a client.

In such circumstances, there is little or no selling to be done. A referral is someone who has made their mind up to use you, and so long as you aren't outrageously expensive or make some other great mistake in your initial meeting with them, it's fairly assured that they're coming on board.

Referrals constitute a huge part of an accountant's experience of winning any kind of new work in the profession, which means that the skills or the 'muscle development' of winning new work isn't exercised too regularly because 82% of the time it's not required.

Understand Selling In Practice by Knowing:

82% of all new clients in a given year that come into an accounting firm come in from a referral source.

A referral is someone who has made their mind up to use you, and so long as you aren't outrageously expensive or make some other great mistake in your initial meeting with them, it's fairly assured that they're coming on board.

8% of new business in our study comes from networking. Again that's professional relationships of different kinds: it includes meetings, conferences, activities, golf days and the like. 7% comes specifically from client centred seminars, and only 3% from what we might determine to be proactive selling.

This means that there is very little exposure historically for practitioners to be able to have developed a selling skillset and that's one of the main reasons why we find it so difficult to win new work proactively.

But let's take a look at it in even more detail than that. Why is it really so difficult to sell?

Well, here's some brief history of the profession, at least as it is relevant to the UK.

From the years 4,000 BC to 1852 AD accountancy began to be established as a concept, a method, a practice and eventually a profession.

 From 1853 through to 1880 we started to see the first organised bodies appearing and a Royal Charter, (which gives rise to the UK term 'chartered accountant'), was granted.

The early organisation of our governing body in the UK, the equivalent of the AICPA in the US, set the standards

Understand Selling In Practice by Knowing:

There is very little exposure historically for practitioners to be able to have developed a selling skillset and that's one of the main reasons why we find it so difficult to win new work proactively.

U.S.P. Points to Ponder

How long have you spent studying and honing your accounting skills?

How long have you spent studying and honing your 'selling' skills?

of professional conduct. And that brings us to the advent of women in accountancy.

During the first world war we see fairly slow progress. During the second world war we see non-practicing members gaining influence within the institute. The first members' handbook is published and so forth.

So that takes us right up from 4,000 BC to 1967. Then ten years on we saw a revolution in 1977 over in the US. A lawyer by the name of Bates decided that the restrictions on his law practice being able to market themselves to win new work placed on them by the code that lawyers adhered to was a direct infringement of his First Amendment rights.

He challenged, and he made the point that under the First Amendment he should be allowed to market himself and win new work proactively. It was a landmark ruling because he won, thus suddenly changing the outlook for the pro-actively dictated growth of professions in a way that they had not seen up until this point.

In 1979 another major event occurred when the Australian super-marketer Paul Dunn had an idea to develop marketing within the accountancy profession. The Results Corporation was formed, which became Results Accounting Systems, which became today's

Understand Selling In Practice by Knowing:

A lawyer by the name of Bates decided that the restrictions on his law practice being able to market themselves to win new work placed on them by the code that lawyers adhered to was a direct infringement of his First Amendment rights.

I had my start in the accounting profession in that timescale towards the late 1990s, and so I personally saw the change that was taking place in public practice.

RAN-ONE Network. The work of those groups changed firms' perceptions of themselves and their ability to win new clients, to grow, to develop, to create infrastructure. The 'game changed' immeasurably.

Now, I had my start in the accounting profession in that timescale towards the late 1990s, and so I personally saw the change that was taking place in public practice.

In 2001 in the UK, there was a significant relaxation in guidelines allowing much greater freedom in professional services marketing. This empowered smaller firms to compete with bigger rivals on a much more even basis.

My reason for outlining all of that history is this: From 4,000 BC to 2014 where we are now, professional selling has never been part of the studied curriculum for a trainee accountant/CPA. So it is not too difficult to understand that proactive selling is something that we perhaps fear and that we struggle to grow the practice in any meaningful way. Marketing, which is now matured in the profession, is able to create those opportunities and many, many marketeers and marketing organisations do a fantastic job of creating opportunities. However, turning those opportunities into clients (closing a deal) is where the hurdle exists.

Understand Selling In Practice by Knowing:

In 2001 in the UK, there was a significant relaxation in guidelines allowing much greater freedom in professional services marketing. This empowered smaller firms to compete with bigger rivals on a much more even basis.

It is not too difficult to understand that proactive selling is something that we perhaps fear and that, as a result, we struggle to grow the practice in any meaningful way.

So, in summary, the reason it's so difficult to sell is actually fourfold.

• Ultimately the profession has never been trained to sell, and therefore the skillset to do so is not something that would necessarily be innate to a technical professional.

• Selling, which is sort of an unknown and perhaps a slightly uncomfortable element of practice management, is stigmatised. We tell ourselves, "I can't do it, I don't know how to do it, I am scared of being able to do it. I see other people doing it and it seems to not be the right fit." And all of these things 'stigmatise' selling in our minds.

• We see ourselves being sold to and 'selling' being presented to us in so many forms, and usually not particularly good forms. Therefore we get an impression or a stereotype of what selling must be like and it just doesn't seem like a fit for a profession like accountancy.

• There's a huge difference between chasing new fees and attracting them. We need to be concentrating on that second element, which is the Law of Attraction. Stage one of mastering the Law of Attraction is to be comfortable with self, which I present here in this guidebook as 'Winning your first client'.

Understand Selling In Practice by Knowing:

We get an impression or a stereotype of what selling must be like and it just doesn't seem like a fit for a profession like accountancy.

There's a huge difference between chasing new fees and attracting them.

5th Piece of Value – Don't Chase New Fees, Attract Them

Let's start this section with two simple definitions to avoid any confusion:

- The Purpose of marketing is to create the opportunity.

- The Purpose of business development (selling) is to convert that opportunity into a paying client.

When we meet with prospective clients—and I say this as someone who has sat in on many hundreds of meetings of this nature—we rarely give potential clients a reason to buy from us that they care about.

There might be a number of reasons that we believe are strong and compelling factors for them considering engaging us, but what about them? What about how *they* feel? What about *their* decision-making factors? What about *their* concerns and objections? That's where the focus needs to be.

If we don't understand the value we deliver beyond traditional compliance work, then how are we going to convince anyone else?

Understand Selling In Practice by Knowing:

---

*We rarely give potential clients
a reason to buy from us that
<u>they</u> care about.*

---

*If we don't understand the
value we deliver beyond
traditional compliance work,
then how are we going to
convince anyone else?*

If we don't believe that we can positively differentiate from any other competing firms, including the incumbent firm the potential client might be with right now, how are we going to stand out from the crowd?

If *we* don't believe we have the solution for them, why are we expecting *them* to believe we have the solution for them?

If you gain nothing else from this book, I would love you to take away this point, embed it deeply and recall it regularly—we are our first client. We have to understand why clients buy from us. We have to understand how businesses and business owners think about their businesses and how our value and our skill set aids their goals, ambitions and strategies.

Once we understand our value, self-confidence stops being a problem in client meetings. Answers to unusual questions occur to us far more promptly as we are freed from worrying about whether we're going to look good or lose the work based on our answer. We change from talking about features (the vehicles of delivery in our firm that perhaps reinforce our technical competence) and we'll focus on benefits, the reasons why this potential client should engage us in order to forward their own goals.

Understand Selling In Practice by Knowing:

If you gain nothing else from this book, I would love you to take away this point, embed it deeply and recall it regularly—we are our first client.

We change from talking about features (the vehicles of delivery in our firm that perhaps reinforce our technical competence) and we'll focus on benefits, the reasons why this potential client should engage us in order to forward their own goals.

So becoming our first client is a process that should happen every single day. In motivational speaking circles I hear it talked about as positive self-talk or affirmations. Whatever system works for you is great, so long as it helps you understand the reality, not some fantasy, but the reality of what you, your firm, your people, your service offering, impacts the wellbeing of a business that you might go and talk to.

Physiology, or in other words body language, is 55% of the impression or perception created by the client about us, regardless of the reality. Therefore we need to be able to positively influence their perception of us and our body language (open arms, relaxed posture more than folded arms, crossed legs) plays a 55% role in achieving that.

The tone of our voice is said to constitute 38% of our client's perception of us.

You can tell when somebody says something to you that they don't believe. You can pick up doubt or insincerity in a voice. That's 38% of the whole picture that is painted of us, so it's a very big deal.

Believe it or not, the actual words we employ and the order in which we employ them to convey and communicate our value is only 7% of the total equation.

Understand Selling In Practice by Knowing:

You can tell when somebody says something to you that they don't believe. You can pick up doubt or insincerity in a voice.

We can really help the business owner we're talking to, and so the tone is positive, engaging and enthusiastic.

So the 'winning the first client' concept comes into its own here in that we understand why we're valuable, so we're relaxed. We can really help the business owner we're talking to, and so the tone is positive, engaging and enthusiastic.

This means that the words must come naturally to us. We know our subject, we know our value, we know what they and their business need because we've been asking those questions and they've been telling us the story of where they've come from, where they are now and where they and their business wish to go.

Getting those skills together gives us the process we need to start winning new work.

U.S.P. Points to Ponder

Name your three closest competitors

1. _____

2. _____

3. _____

What do you offer that they don't?

_____

_____

_____

Why engage your firm rather than any of your competitors?

_____

_____

_____

6th Piece of Value – It's about time to realise that value is not about time

When I look back on the research that has been conducted by various groups as to the biggest obstacles accounting firms cite to growing their practice, 50% said creating opportunities, 25% said knowing how to close deals, and the remainder said having self-confidence in presenting and then being able to positively differentiate from their competition.

It's the final category of having self- confidence in presenting and then being able to positively differentiate from their competition that dictates how easy or difficult the other elements of creating and closing opportunities become for the firm.

Let's not sell, let's attract.

Selling—that stigmatised thing, that thing we're unfamiliar with, that thing that we haven't been trained to do, that thing that we feel uncomfortable with and perhaps relate to negative experiences—means pushing something on someone. We have something to sell and we say, "Do you want this?" That's selling. "Here's all the reasons why you should want this, we'll do you a deal today if you take this, have this, buy the stuff." That's selling in an exceptionally basic form.

Understand Selling In Practice by Knowing:

It's the final category of having self-confidence in presenting and then being able to positively differentiate from their competition that dictates how easy or difficult the other elements of creating and closing opportunities become for the firm.

Let's not sell, let's attract.

Attracting is demonstrating your expertise gently and professionally. It's the ability to build a relationship, and understand the needs of the business owner you're talking to because you've created rapport so that they feel comfortable in explaining their outlook to you.It's demonstrating without being pushy in any way that your value meets those needs and wants, and then simply allowing them the opportunity to come on board with you if that's something they want to do.

If joining your firm as its newest client is not something that they want to do, no problem. We appreciate their time and we'd ask to keep in touch with them, and when the opportunity comes to talk again we'd love to be able to do so. In the interim, their choosing not to join us is not a concern for us, because we are so confident and assured having 'won the first client' that morning that we understand our value, that our value is attractive to everybody we see. We're not going to have a problem getting clients on board here—we aren't desperately in need of your business, Mr. or Mrs. Potential Client.

We know there's nothing worse than a professional appearing to be desperate to win some work, and we're not that person today. We are a self-assured, confident, very engaging individual that has the solution to the needs that the prospect is outlining, and if they would like to

Understand Selling In Practice by Knowing:

We're not going to have a problem getting clients on board here—we aren't desperately in need of your business, Mr. or Mrs. Potential Client.

We know there's nothing worse than a professional appearing to be desperate to win some work, and we're not that person today.

take that opportunity we're offering to them—great; and if they don't, there's no problem whatsoever.

'Selling' is the prescriptive delivery of something and a choice to be made. Attracting is a demonstration of how our value meets their needs and giving them the option of taking it or not.

The skill in professional selling and understanding selling in practice is to move from this hesitancy that we have in appearing to be 'pushy' through to being able to be genuinely interested in a business regardless of the outcome of that meeting.

As contrast and context to this point, please bear in mind that still to this day over 90% of accounting firms are delivering the compliance work required by law for their clients to an acceptable standard, but not going beyond that.

If the marketing revolution in accounting has demonstrated anything, it has proven that a large percentage of many firms' clients want something more than compliance, but have two beliefs.

- that the firm either doesn't provide what they are looking for so they won't ask;

  or worse,

Understand Selling In Practice by Knowing:

Selling' is the prescriptive delivery of something and a choice to be made. Attracting is a demonstration of how our value meets their needs and giving them the option of taking it or not.

The skill in professional selling and understanding selling in practice is to move from this hesitancy that we have in appearing to be 'pushy' through to being able to be genuinely interested in a business regardless of the outcome of that meeting.

- that the firm doesn't provide what they are looking for beyond compliance so they'll look to a different firm for help.

We need to break down the unspoken barriers in our clients' minds, to be able to create deeper relationships that are ultimately more altruistic and yet profitable for us. That gives us the opportunity then to really develop the practice in terms of the engagements that we throw into our work in progress mix.

We need to buy into ourselves, we need to be able to say 'I get this, I get why a business should engage our firm'. 'I get what the competition are doing and I get why we're superior in terms of what the client needs'.

That's the first client won.

If we can close that sale we can close any sale, because we don't need to try to 'sell'. We need to be ourselves, self-assured professionals with huge value to offer, invested in building relationships.

Understand Selling In Practice by Knowing:

> *We need to break down the unspoken barriers in our clients' minds, to be able to create deeper relationships that are ultimately more altruistic and yet profitable for us.*

> *We need to buy into ourselves, we need to be able to say 'I get this, I get why a business should engage our firm'. 'I get what the competition are doing and I get why we're superior in terms of what the client needs'.*

7th Piece of Value – Scheduling + Implementing x Skill x Knowledge = New Fees

You may be thinking right now, "Well, very good, Martin, but we have finite time. We're very, very busy people and we need to get business in the door, and therefore creation of opportunity becomes the issue."

Regardless of whether we've got twenty opportunities on our plate today or none, when the next one comes along we can't afford to be anything other than confident, comfortable, assured relationship builders who have tremendous value to offer. Because people will see that body language, those voice tones and hear those words and it will be attractive. They will want to get to know more—they'll want to be able to look at options. They'll want to know what you'll charge, and they'll want to know what they'll get for what you charge.

As the accounting profession increasingly goes towards a scenario where partners need to employ professional selling skills, then the more understanding we have as to why people choose us other than being recommended, the more competitive advantage we will have.

So here are three everyday disciplines to start your proactive efforts to grow the practice with the right kind of

Understand Selling In Practice by Knowing:

Regardless of whether we've got twenty opportunities on our plate today or none, when the next one comes along we can't afford to be anything other than confident, comfortable, assured relationship builders who have tremendous value to offer.

As the accounting profession increasingly goes towards a scenario where partners need to employ professional selling skills, then the more understanding we have as to why people choose us other than being recommended, the more competitive advantage we will have.

work at the right kind of fee without spending huge amounts of money and time on either.

1. Let's close the first sale to ourselves every single day, before we even get started. Let's prepare for our meetings having won the first client and knowing what value we can offer.

2. Let's always allow in our diary, wherever possible, two slots for every appointment we need to make with each business in case they can't make the first one we offer. There's always an alternative, so that when they can't do that first date we don't lose control of the opportunity—we simply give them an alternative.

3. Let's schedule all follow ups that have to be done. Whether it's debriefing our marketing team after a meeting, actually scheduling the next meeting in the diary, or preparing and rehearsing how we will present a proposal document to them, let's make sure that we never leave those initial meetings with prospective clients without having our second meeting in the diary—or our third meeting or our fourth meeting, whatever it may be. Let's make sure all appointments are scheduled and we allow time to prepare for them, to debrief after them, and to attend them. Otherwise we're rushing and we're just diminishing our own chances of conversion.

Understand Selling In Practice by Knowing:

Let's close the first sale to ourselves every single day.

Let's always allow in our diary, wherever possible, two slots for every appointment we need to make with each business in case they can't make the first one we offer.

Let's schedule all follow ups that have to be done.

8th Piece Of Value – Compliance Sells on Fee, Advisory Sells on Value

I've spent a long time in this guidebook asking you to believe in yourself, get your potential clients to open up to you and to demonstrate to them what outcomes in their personal and professional lives working with you and your firm would create.

Now here's a checklist for you to run through before you begin your next business development initiative, and before each new business appointment that you have. You don't need theory. You need the habit of implementation and practice. So I wish you every success in making both a reality.

❏ Understand the difference between marketing and business development

❏ Firmly map out your plans for growth

❏ Assign yourself to become accountable to someone

❏ Have them evaluate you

❏ Decide what your value is relative to each individual new opportunity when you meet with them for the first time

❏ Decide whether you believe in you

❏ Decide whether you would buy from you

❏ Decide to have a walk-away price for every deal

❏ Decide why you and your firm are *better* than your competitors for each prospect you see, not just different

❏ Schedule specific, non-interruptible time in your diary to proactively work on business development initiatives

Before you present yourself to a potential client, are you honestly comfortable with:

❏ How you treated your family members recently?

❏ How well you've been striving to hit any personal goals that you might have set yourself?

❏ How you've dealt with employees and clients recently?

❏ What you did when no-one could see you?

❏ What you think about, if it were to be made public?

❏ The way you present yourself visually?

❏ The way you present yourself verbally?

❏ The work you do for your clients?

❏ Yourself, to the extent that if you met you, you'd be impressed?

❏ How much preparation you've invested into this meeting?

You're now ready to build the pipeline of opportunities for your firm.

About the Author

Martin Bissett is the founder of The Upward Spiral partnership Ltd. (USP), the UK-based consulting firm that specializes in the implementation of professional selling and leadership skills in the next generation of accounting professionals.

Previously, Martin served ten years on the board of the directors of the UK's leading provider of high-quality new business appointments for accountancy firms. There, he held the responsibility for the nurture and organic growth of the organization's new client base, including six of the UK's top 30 firms of accountants.

Martin became fascinated by the apparent juxtaposition of partners not vocalizing what they were looking for in terms of an accomplished skill set from their potential future partners and their managers not asking to discover what that skill set included, despite wanting to reach that very position. In a profession with a supposed "Succession Crisis" on the horizon, this apparent "stand off" struck him as curious.

This has led Upward Spiral Partnership to personally interview several hundred partners and managers in the US and UK to learn what partners are looking for and how the managers see their own future in the firm. There are, of course, firms who have addressed this issue already, and their initiatives have also been captured.

The result of the research, including both the consensus and the exceptions to the general opinion, is called "Passport to Partnership." This study provides the highlights of each factor that the majority of partners interviewed use as their criteria when evaluating whether someone in their organization can make it to the top.

As a result of the combination of his experience, intellectual property and this proprietary research, Martin now consults with accounting firms in the UK, Europe and the USA.

He can be reached in the United Kingdom by telephone at 07708 922622 or by email at martin@upwardspiralpartnership.co.uk.

ACTIONABLE INTELLIGENCE FOR THE TAX, ACCOUNTING & FINANCE COMMUNITY

About CPA Trendlines

Tax, accounting and finance professionals worldwide rely on CPA Trendlines to deliver the actionable intelligence they need to identify and act on emerging issues and opportunities.

We specialize in high-quality, concise executive briefings designed to help busy professionals improve their organizations, advance their careers, and enhance their lives. Our reports are relevant, timely and to-the-point, providing only the most essential, most practical, information. Many are readable in under an hour and are immediately actionable.

Visit us at cpatrendlines.com.

Rick Telberg
President / CEO
CPA Trendlines

Store.CPATrendlines
THE PROFESSIONAL RESOURCES PROFESSIONALS NEED

More at Store.CPATrendlines.com

Made in the USA
Middletown, DE
23 April 2015